# The Man Who Lived On Main Street

## Stories By and About Sol Schulman

Collected and Edited by
Jan Schochet and
Sharon Fahrer

Published by History@Hand Publishing
333 Montford Avenue
Asheville, North Carolina 28801

Designed by Alan Moss

Manufactured in the United States of America

10 9 8 7 6 5 4 3 2 1

Library of Congress Control Number 2003114150

Includes bibliographical references and index.

ISBN 0-9746424-0-1

# Dedication

This book is dedicated to the Schulman family:

To Lillian Schulman, Sol's wife of forty-two years.

To Herbert Schulman and his wife Norma Yospin Schulman,
their daughter Leslie and granddaughter Kelsey.

To David Schulman, his wife Denissa Andrews Schulman
and their children Stephanie and Nate.

# Acknowledgments

We have a long list of people we would like to thank who helped us along the way in creating this book. We apologize if we've left anyone out. We haven't meant to, and we thank all of you.

We appreciate the generous help of the Schulmans—Sol, David and Herbert. We also thank Gin Moses, whom Sol has called the daughter he never had. We thank Susan Lewis for providing us with photos and stories about the three Jewish families in Sylva (the Schulmans, the Lessings and the Karps) in the first half of the 1900s. We thank Mr. Schulman's caretakers—Elizabeth Franks, Dick Buchanan and Barry Moody—and all those who answered the phones of the folks we interviewed and made sure we got in touch with them—Reg Moody's daughter, Mary, and Gin Moses' husband, Harry, among them. We thank all those who told us their stories. We wish that we could have used all of them. The names of everyone interviewed are listed in Appendix C.

We especially appreciate the help of Livingston Kelley and his family who made suggestions, helped with photocopying and even provided a relatively quiet place to record when the last days of Schulman's proved too raucous for us to make a clear recording. We appreciate the help of the librarians who made our work easier—Becky Kornegay, George Frizzell and Priscilla Proctor at Western Carolina University's Hunter Library; Michael Cartwright and Tracy Fitzmaurice who researched questions we had and Mary Wilson who provided us with a quiet place to record Dr. El Bayadi, all of the Sylva Public Library; Helen Wykle, Director of Special Collections at Ramsey Library at the University of North Carolina at Asheville (UNCA); and Ann Wright and Zoe Rhine at Pack Library in Asheville, North Carolina, who loaned us field recording equipment.

We couldn't have accomplished much of anything without the work of our patient tape transcribers, Caroline Mason and Helen O'Connor, and we thank them. We appreciate Andrew Goldberg's treks to Sylva to pick up materials for us. We thank Wayne Erbsen for his help with information on publishing. And we thank Ruth Savoca, our tireless reader, and Vic Fahrer.

Thanks go also to Vice-Chancellor Clifford Metcalf, who supported this project. In addition, we thank Dianne Lynch of Chancellor Bardo's office at Western Carolina University (Western or WCU) who forwarded to us the Chancellor's moving speech that is in Appendix A of this book. We are grateful to the support and help of *The Sylva Herald,* particularly Steve Gray, along with Lynn Hotaling, Rose Hooper and Cary Phillips. We also are indebted to Marsha Crites whose idea sparked this publication and who had the vision to help make it a reality.

**Gabardine Suit Sale**

NOT PICKED OVERS, NOT BROKEN SIZES, NOT UNWANTED STYLES, BUT—LOVELY CHOICE FASHIONS FROM ONE OF OUR REGULAR MANUFACTURERS, BOUGHT AT THE END OF THE SEASON AT DRASTIC REDUCTIONS! AND PASSED ON TO YOU AT THE SAME SAVINGS ! ! !

**ONLY $15.00**

**SALE STARTS TODAY**

**DON'T WAIT – QUANTITY LIMITED**

Sizes 10-20 . . . Gorgeous colors . . . Lovely styles
Choose from Black - Skipper - Red - Yellow - Grey - Navy
Toast and Novelty Worsteds

**SCHULMAN'S**
**Dept. Store**

We Feature Only Nationally Known Quality Brands

---

*Schulman's*

**FOR THE BEST IN SHOES!**

THE FLORSHEIM STEPPER

Versatile little sandal of finest calfskin . . . so soft and light you hardly know your weaving shoes!

Color
Twenty Karat Calf
Sizes 5 to 11
AAAA to C widths

**$16.95**

---

**Accent on Embroidery**

Embroidery shapes the bodice to new perfection in this charming pair. Washable, fast color, wrinkle resistant "CULTURED COTTON," a Rubie Levine product.
Left: Rolled collar. Bodice embroidered all over in open nylon thread. Unpressed pleated skirt all around. In periwinkle blue, moss green, rouge red, navy.
Sizes 5-7-9-11-13-15 .......... $10.95

Right: Embroidered bodice with bow and piping at waist. Graceful, shirred skirt in moss green, periwinkle blue, tangerine, turquoise.
Sizes 5-7-9-11-13-15 .......... $8.95

You Saw Them in SEVENTEEN

*for* EASY LIVING

Here's a new CLASSIC LADY that's so easy to wear . . . so easy to care for because it's smartly fashioned of a washable, linen-like rayon. The cross-over bodice is enhanced by sparkling jewelled buttons . . . the side-draped skirt flattering the figure. Choose the "matchstick" design in pink, aqua, lilac or navy; choose solid tones of pink, aqua, periwinkle or navy. Sizes 12½ to 24½.

Classic Lady

**$10.95**

**SCHULMAN'S**

Phone 151 Main Street

# Table of Contents

# Foreward

Late in 2002, merchant Sol Schulman retired at age ninety after seventy years of shop-keeping at Schulman's Department Store in the small mountain town of Sylva, North Carolina. After closing the store because of poor health, Schulman donated the store's clothing, shoes and accessories to the WestCare Health Systems Foundation to sell to benefit the local hospital system. In a series of well-attended sale days, the hospital's foundation benefited greatly from his contribution.

This was but one of scores of charitable acts and gifts offered during his life in Sylva. In his words, "When you are able to give to some person, some family or some important cause, it blesses the beneficiary and the giver." In his view, Mr. Schulman feels blessed to be a blessing.

Sol Schulman was a founding member of the Jackson County Community Foundation, which began in 1992 as an affiliate of the statewide North Carolina Community Foundation. This foundation was established to help people and organizations build permanent endowment funds for the charitable causes most important to them. The North Carolina Community Foundation also acts as a catalyst to enhance philanthropy in all its forms in the communities where it works throughout the state.

As the Jackson County Community Foundation's most generous member and friend to date, Schulman has been eager not only to get the money invested, but also to see it distribute income to the local causes the Foundation was meant to benefit.

This year, the Jackson County Community Foundation is collaborating with Mr. Schulman, his family and friends, independent historians Sharon Fahrer and Jan Schochet, and the downtown redevelopment project Sylva Partners in Renewal (S.P.I.R) to publish some of the best stories told by and about Sol Schulman and his active life in Sylva. Funds raised from the sale of this book will begin the Sol and Lillian Schulman Family Endowment for Downtown Sylva. Distributions each year will help Sylva Partners in Renewal to beautify and revitalize this small mountain town in Western North Carolina.

We hope you enjoy reading about this delightful and generous man as much as we have enjoyed collecting and publishing the stories.

Marsha S. Crites, Senior Associate
for Special Projects
North Carolina Community Foundation
July 28, 2003

Copyright © Asheville Post Card Co.

# Sylva, North Carolina

Sylva is a pleasant small town of three square miles nestled in the Blue Ridge mountains between Balsam Gap (elevation 3,343 ft.) and Cherokee, North Carolina. It was chartered on March 9, 1889, just twenty-three years and six days before Sol Schulman was born. The current population is 2,300.

**Distance in miles to:**

- Atlanta, GA - 149
- Asheville, NC - 48
- Charlotte, NC - 130
- Greenville, SC - 56
- Knoxville, TN - 92
- Washington, DC - 520
- New York City - 750

**Distance to places mentioned in this book:**

- Canton, NC - 24
- Orangeburg, SC - 186
- Reidsville, NC - 210
- High Point, NC - 186
- Cherryville, NC - 103
- Bryson City, NC - 13
- Franklin, NC - 16

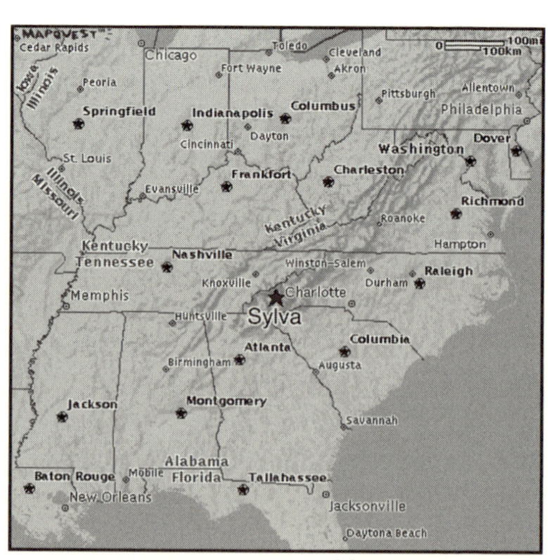

© Copyright MapQuest.com, Inc

# Introduction

How did two Asheville women end up collecting and editing this book of stories about Sol Schulman? We were starting to work on an in-depth project about Asheville's downtown history and Asheville's Jewish community, and we thought it important to meet with various people who could give us input.

We had an interesting five-hour meeting with David Schulman at his Asheville home, and as we were leaving Jan and David exchanged inquiries about their parents. David knows Jan's father and, in fact, has interviewed him. Jan only knew of David's father, but he responded that, after seventy years in his store, his father was closing it. He mentioned that his father had donated the stock to WestCare Health Systems Foundation which was selling it as a fundraiser.

Jan said that she imagined there were a lot of stories after seventy years. And David said, "You know, that's exactly what the volunteers running the sale have said—that all kinds of people are coming in telling stories. About Dad, about the store, about things they bought in the store."

Bingo! We looked at each other and said, "We've got to get those stories. No one else in the region has run a store for seventy years!" And we quickly made plans to go to Sylva.

Before we went, Jan told a good friend about going to Schulman's. Her husband, who had graduated from Western, immediately launched into a long story about "good old Sol" selling him his first suit. She thought he was being a little disrespectful by calling Mr. Schulman by his first name (he said Sol had told him to) and that he was overdoing it a little by going on and on about the man. But when we got to Sylva and started asking people about Mr. Schulman, we got pretty much the same response from everyone. They all had a story, and they mostly couldn't say enough about the man.

Even today, after more than thirty stories, Jan was at her veterinarian in Asheville, and the X-ray technician told her she graduated from Western. Jan asked her if she ever went into Sylva and if she knew Sol Schulman. "Oh of course, and my mother-in-law was absolutely devastated that the store had to close. She shopped there all the time," she said.

We were lucky enough on that first visit to talk to the folks at *The Sylva Herald* about our collecting project and that they decided to run a half-page article about the store closing. It mentioned we would be collecting stories the last two days of the store's existence. We were also lucky enough to have people waiting for us when we came back and that one of them was Marsha

Crites of the Jackson County Community Foundation. She mentioned she'd always wanted to do a fundraiser for the Foundation in the form of a book of stories about Sol Schulman. Sharon told her, "We can do that!"

So here is that book.

For all those people who lived in Sylva all those years it seemed as though Sol never left Main Street, that he was the epitome of the small town merchant—always there, no matter how far off you went. Hence the title, "The Man Who Lived on Main Street."

Just a few notes on reading this book. We have presented the stories very close to the original way in which people told them to us. We have not rewritten them, as we wanted them to survive in their truest form.

In some instances, in order to make for easier reading, we have deleted words, phrases and sentences that were about a different subject or that were repetitive. These deletions are noted by ellipses, a series of three dots. If there is a sentence ending followed by a deletion, there is a period and then an ellipsis (totaling four dots). In this way the reader knows the material was edited. We also have added bracketed words and phrases necessary for the story to read easily, as people often don't speak as exactly as they write.

We are grateful to have had the opportunity to work on this book, to meet so many wonderful folks in the Sylva area and to get to know Sol and his family and friends.

Jan Schochet
Sharon Fahrer
Asheville, North Carolina
July 2003

# PART I
# BACKGROUND

# Sol's Family Story

Sol Schulman was born in New York City on March 15, 1912, the youngest of eight children. His parents were immigrants from Lithuania and his father, Sam, worked as a cutter in a New York garment factory. When he was eight years old, his mother became ill and was hospitalized, so he was sent to live with an older married sister in Orangeburg, South Carolina. From that time on, Sol was raised to be a shop owner. His sister and her husband ran a clothing store, and Sol was expected to work there. When he was only twelve years old, they even left him to watch the store while they went out of town on a buying trip.

His father eventually moved from New York to Reidsville, North Carolina, north of Greensboro, and opened a store. Sol moved there to live with his father, and he graduated from Reidsville High School in 1929. Sol's father later moved on to Cherryville, North Carolina, near Charlotte, to start a business. It was the Depression, but Sol's father and two older sisters began investing in real estate.

In 1932 they built a store in western North Carolina on Main Street in the mountain town of Sylva. It sat empty for six months until one day Sam Schulman sent nineteen-year-old Sol to see if he could rent it or sell it. Sol got off the train in Sylva, looked around and liked what he saw—the mountains, the town and the people. He preferred, as he tells it, to be "a big fish in a small pond, rather than a small fish in a big pond." He stayed and opened Schulman's Department Store (see page 7 for the story of how Sol rented the building).

Lillian, Sol's wife of forty-two years, worked alongside him in Schulman's, often urging him to "just give it to them, Sol" if a customer could not afford to pay. Her measure of wealth was in happiness, not money. Their two sons, Herbert and David, also grew up in Schulman's and worked there until each opened his own business.

Other brothers and sisters in Sol's family also owned retail clothing stores located in various North Carolina towns including, Canton, Hendersonville, Bessemer City and Marion and, for a short period, Franklin and Bryson City. Theirs is the story of many Jewish families that lived in small towns in the south. Some came as peddlers, and as they became more affluent, they opened shops. Some came for their health. Still others came to join relatives who already lived in the region, while some just wanted to escape large cities. All saw the South as a fine place to bring up a family and have a business. This is how many Jewish families became southerners, proud of their towns and contributors to their communities.

So, at the young age of nineteen, Sol opened Schulman's Department store. On the first day, a small group of local men arrived before business hours. Sol thought they came to welcome him, but instead, they told him he would never make it. Were they ever wrong! Seventy years later, here is a wonderful collection of stories about Sylva and Schulman's Department store's seven decades of success.

# PART II
# Stories

# Chapter 1 – Sol Comes to Sylva

## HOW SOL ARRIVED IN SYLVA

*Sol:*

There was depression on. I mean a *real* depression.

So I came up here to see if I couldn't sell it, lease it or rent it [building on Main Street]. Stayed about a week and I liked the place. I liked the people. Liked the whole area.

So I called my dad up and I said, "I've got the building rented."

"You have? Wonderful! Who is it? Is he good?"

"Sure he's good."

"Is he honest?"

"Sure, he's honest."

"Will he pay the rent?"

"Sure, he'll pay the rent."

"How much you getting?"

[He was only asking $50 a month, Sol said "$55."]

He again said, "Wonderful! What's his name?"

I said, "When I get home I'll tell you."

I got home and he said, "Who did you rent it to?"

And I said, "Me!"

"What? A nineteen-year-old pischer [Yiddish for "a little squirt"] taking a store with [the] Depression on? People not even making a living and you're going to open a store?"

"Yeah."

"Well, I don't think you should, but if you need some help, I'll be glad to help you."

"I don't need any help, but I appreciate it."

## HOW SOL STOCKED THE STORE

*Sol:*

So I decided to open a store. . . . What do I do for merchandise? I need to get merchandise. He [father] said, "Take whatever you want to start." There wasn't enough in those days to go around. And I didn't want anybody else's merchandise. I wanted my own.

So I went to [the] Baltimore Bargain House and I went up to the credit manager. I said, "I'm opening another store and I want to buy some merchandise and I need some credit."

He looked up my dad's credit. It wasn't good, it wasn't bad. . . . [He was a] slow payer. He said, "So how much merchandise do you want?"

I said, "I need five thousand dollars, at least."

He said, "Go over there and get what you want."

They had everything in there—shoes, pants, shirts—men's, women's, children's. So he gave me credit for five thousand dollars and I picked out the merchandise and he shipped it to me. When it came, I needed two hundred and twelve dollars to pay for freight. I didn't have the money. So I went to one of my brothers and said I need the money.

[He said] OK. He loaned me the money.

I had the merchandise for about two or three weeks. . . . Nobody around here was selling good merchandise. Florsheim shoes, Stetson hats. . . . So I sent him [creditor] a check at that time, five hundred dollars on account. And I said, "You made a mistake. On the invoice it says I.S. Schulman [Sol's father]. It should be S. Schulman."

The credit manager called me up and said, "What's the matter? . . . Some man came here opening another store."

. . . "[You] must have misunderstood. It's S. Schulman."

I had the goods, what's he going to do? Call me a pischer [Yiddish for "a little squirt"], what're you going to do? So I had the goods and finally paid him.

*Eds. note: Baltimore Bargain House (BBH as it was known) supplied Jewish peddlers throughout the South, then as the peddlers became prosperous enough to open a store, BBH supplied those stores. BBH later became American Wholesale Corporation. [According to David Schulman.]*

## HOW SOL STAYED AFLOAT

*Jack Hinson:*

And I said, "Sol you opened this store five years before I was born and you're as healthy as I am right now. You don't show your age." And I just couldn't believe it.

And he began to tell me the circumstances. . . . If Roosevelt hadn't closed the bank, he might not have made it because he owed some money. But he told the people he couldn't get it out of the bank because it was closed. Which he couldn't.

And he didn't have enough in the bank, but he didn't tell them that. And he couldn't get it out of the bank. But then it [the bank] was opened back up. Well, then he had enough [money] where he could [pay them]. But it was just so close.

He almost went under so many times. But he kept bobbling and coming on back. And it's certainly a story of persistence and endurance and genuine compassion for people.

## WELCOMING COMMITTEE

*Sol:*

Things were real bad everywhere. And [the first day] a delegation came—about six or eight guys—came to the store and knocked on the door. I hadn't even opened up yet.

One of the men said, "Mr. Schulman? Is that your name? Your daddy here?"

I said, "My daddy's not here."

"Who opened this store?"

"Me."

"You opened this store?"

"Yeah."

"We've just come to tell you something."

I thought they were going to say, "We wish you well."

"You'll never make it."

A little later I said, "Gee whiz. They started me off good to tell me not to open. I'm here with all this merchandise and they tell me not to open." It wasn't very nice of them to say. that. But they did.

And just for spite, I did good!

## BACK THEN

*Sol:*

Well, the thing is, you had a lot of stores here at that time, but most of them [sold] work clothes, work shoes, work boots. I opened up with a little better merchandise. Suits, good shoes, good hats. Nobody around here was selling that.

Although there wasn't much business, there was plenty for one to two stores. So I did good.

## A DOCTOR ON A HORSE

*Sol:*

When I first came here in 1933 . . . they didn't have a . . . real nice . . . hotel here . . . so I rented an apartment up above one of the stores downtown. In the middle of the night—might have been one or two o'clock in the morning—I heard some shooting.

I thought maybe I ate too much that night. Thought I was dreaming. [He looked out the window.]

A big man was [naked] on a horse, on a white horse. I thought, "Am I nuts or am I dreaming?"

I wasn't dreaming. . . . It was [the town doctor]. He must have weighed three hundred pounds. I don't see how he got on top of a horse. But he was coming down through Main Street shooting a gun.

That was [in the] first three months I came. I said, "Oooh, wonderful town. Better pay your rent here."

## THE ARCHITECT

*Sol:*

The man who designed this house only made three blueprints in his lifetime. . . . There was a depression on and I saw his name in the paper. [He was Charles Parker, the man who designed The Grove Arcade, an indoor market place and office building in Asheville.]

. . . Called him up. . . . Told him to call me if he was in town. . . . He did it, too. . . . He couldn't get any work. It was the Depression. . . . He was a good architect.

## THE BUILDER

*Sol:*

. . . Years ago every town had a real good builder. Usually a good man with plain common sense. Not too much education, but he knew his business. So I wanted to build a house. I was here for five years before I was married. . . . [Someone told me to] get a hold of him and he'll build you the best house you ever saw.

. . . I didn't call him. Not many folks had a telephone in those days—lucky to have a pair of shoes in those days. So I called up a guy and had word sent to him that I wanted to talk to him.

He came by the store and said, "What can I do for you?" Very crude.

So I said, "I want you to build me a house."

He shook his head and walked out.

I thought, "That's funny." Usually they say there's a reason why. There's no reason why. He just said no. It bothered me a lot and I couldn't say why. Had a reason in my head why, maybe.

Three months later the same thing happened. I wanted to still see if I could get him to build me a house. Called him in and he said, "Nope," and walked out. Not much you could do if he won't build. . . .

Then another six months later, I see him on the street and I said, "Come by tomorrow. I want to talk to you. Why don't you want to build me a house?"

"Well, I just don't want to build one." Then he said, "I'll tell you what I'll do. I'll build you a house on one condition. Let me do all the buying, all the hiring; make it according to your plan . . . if you just don't interfere with my work."

I said, "I don't want to interfere with your work. I won't interfere with your work. I want you to build the house. . . ."

Well, he got the job. And he built this house. Did a good job on it. Asked me to go around about four months after I hired him. "Everything's fine. I want you and your wife to come by the house and see if everything's OK. If it's OK, maybe you can pay me and we'll be through."

I'd been going by every day after we closed the store in the evening. We liked what we saw. Said to him, "You did a good job. I want to pay you, and I appreciate it." So I paid him whatever it was worth.

And I said, "Now I want you to have a good Hart-Schaffner-Marx suit, a good overcoat, pair of Florsheim shoes, a Stetson hat."

"I can't afford that! No. I can't buy all that. You want me to pay for it by the week?"

I said, "Who said anything about paying for it? I want you to have one."

"You mean you're going to give me one?"

"Yep. I'm going to give you one."

You see in those days everything was cheap. I paid him what he had said and in the pants—there were four pockets—two in the front and two in the back—I put a hundred dollar bill in each pocket. His eyes got as big around as saucers.

"What's this for?"

"It's a bonus."

"What's a bonus?"

"A little extra."

"I can't understand it. Sure is nice of you. I'll tell you one thing—if you ever see any Jews who want to build a house, send 'em to me."

## POSTSCRIPT

*Sol:*

The reason he didn't want to build, because he never had built for Jews and he thought Jews had tails and horns sticking out. He was a wonderful builder.

He said, "Now, I don't do anything for free. I get paid for what I do." This was before he took the job. "I make thirty-five cents an hour. I do the supervising. I don't just stand around and watch other people. I do plumbing and wiring, a little bit of everything."

And he said, "Now, my next man under me makes twenty cents an hour."

"OK."

"And the man who does the common labor, the one who does the most work, the one who picks up the dirt with a shovel"—they didn't have mechanical machines then, they had a horse and scoops to scoop out the dirt—"he gets ten cents an hour."

And people talk about hard times. But he did a good job.

# Chapter 2 – Sylva Stories

## EARLY SYLVA

*Lloyd Cowan:*

It's all timing. You can go in business and the timing had better be right or you won't make it. They started this dam up here at Glenville. Those Yankees came down from New Jersey and they was used to nice clothes. Our local people were still wearing overalls, dungarees and hunting clothes, you know. Maybe a Sunday hat, a Sunday dress that they wore all their life.

So Sol came here and says, "Hey, we believe we've got people who want some nice dress clothes." So he put in what you call "advertised brands." That excited people. . . . So he's got all those advertised brands that people knew of, but the price was . . . higher than just your normal work and hunting clothes. People were wearing overalls seven days a week, even to Sunday school or church. I wore overalls until I was grown.

But Sol came here and, of course, being urban-oriented, his family out of Statesville by way of New York, up north. And he knew nothing about hunting or fishing or camping or working. . . . Sol didn't know what a pitchfork even looked like, you know, but he knew how to sell and merchandise the clothing.

So he comes here in the early thirties when they started the Glenville Dam. And most of those engineers and people up there, many of them were from up north. And they were people who were used to dress clothes and nice clothes. Most people here traded at the old Sylva Supply. They'd buy their work clothes and their groceries and feed and fertilizers, and what have you, from the old Sylva Supply down here on the corner. And most of them had it charged and paid later.

But Sol didn't sell nothing on the credit. He brought his advertised merchandise in, and if somebody wanted a nice gabardine suit or Red Cross shoes, they were compelled to come to Sol's, because Sylva Supply and the downtown stores didn't have it. They were still carrying work clothes and hunting clothes. So he just literally just hit it with the Glenville Dam up here—Fontana Dam at Glenville—there for a few years, then went right through that and about the time that was completed, here comes World War II.

And of course that brought traffic and prosperity. And so many things back then were rationed. . . . So Sol, he was known as the dress clothing store west of Asheville. So Sol not only had the market in Jackson County, he was well known throughout Western North Carolina for his advertised brands and his tall and big size clothing, his oversize and odd sizes. And his price was no factor. He put the price he thought was right for that merchandise, and he didn't barter with anybody. He got his price.

But when I first heard of Sol, I was just a boy. My sister worked here [in Schulman's Store]. Then later, as I've told you, I was graduating from the old Webster High School in 1941 and I needed a suit. I'd never worn a suit. Eighteen years old and I came right there, to that rack where those dresses are now, and Sol fitted me in a nice, tan one hundred percent wool gabardine three-piece suit. Boy was I dressed up. So I got my first pair of swim trunks from Sol at age sixteen, then I got my first three-piece suit from him when I was eighteen. Then the war broke out.

## JACKSON FURNITURE THOROUGHFARE

*Livingston Kelley:*

Well, let me tell you another tale about Mr. Schulman. I worked in Jackson Furniture Company which was next door to Mr. Schulman's store. And our stairs going from Front Street to Back Street was a thoroughfare. Everybody went up and down the stairs going from Front Street to Back.

And the owner of the store, Mr. Reed, he was sitting back of his desk. And Mr. Schulman came up the stairs from Back Street. Of course, this is a furniture store with large merchandise. And Mr. Schulman comes up the stairs and in through the store and out towards the front.

And Mr. Reed says, "What's wrong Sol? Did you not find anything you wanted?"

Mr. Schulman comes back just like that (snaps fingers) and said, "No, it was all too big to get into my pockets. I'm going to the dime store."

## GIN MOSES SAYS

*Gin Moses:*

And I just went and applied for a job with him and been with him ever since. That was twenty-seven years ago. Twenty-seven. And my son was . . . really young. He grew up in the store. He would go upstairs and he would rig up this little thing and watch television.

As he grew up, he wanted a suit like Mr. S. That's what he called him. He was chunky. So, he [Sol] called everywhere and ordered him a little suit.

## THE MOSES FAMILY CHAUFFEUR

*Gin Moses:*

. . . As time went on . . . Mr. S. had bought a new Cadillac. My son Todd—he was in the eighth grade so he wanted Mr. S. to chauffeur him in the Cadillac to the eighth grade prom. So, he [Sol] borrowed David's [Sol's son] leather chauffeur's cap . . . and he took them to the prom. He had more fun than they did.

. . . And at his twelfth grade prom he [Todd] took a girl. He [Sol] had another new Cadillac and this time Todd wanted to borrow it. I said, "No, you have to ask [him] that," and I had just bought a Honda, a new Honda.

He said, "Oh, no big deal," Mr. S did. "I'll just drive your Honda around the block to home and Todd can come and get the car for the prom."

So he loaned Todd the car for his twelfth grade prom, but he drove up in [his] garage in my Honda and it has all these little buttons and he got locked in it and he couldn't get out. So, he said he thought he was going to die before somebody found him. . . . Every button, every mirror was turned every which way 'cause he is brilliant with numbers and making money, but you know he's not a mechanic (laughs). So anyway, that worked out all right.

## GENE AUSTIN'S CAR STORY

*David Schulman:*

Gene Austin taught Herbert and me to drive a car because my father was always busy in the store. Gene would take Herbert and me fishing, too, for the same reason. While teaching Herbert to drive, Gene had him drive around Chipper Curve near the old Mead Plant and right by the wood flume [water filled channel to transport logs]. Herbert drove so close to the edge of the road that Gene leaned almost into his lap. I was in the back seat, and had to fall on the floor of the opposite side of the car as Herbert took the curve hoping we could tilt the car enough so it wouldn't fall into the flume. We didn't fall in.

## GENE AUSTIN GOT SHOT

*Sol:*

When he got shot [hunting], I found out he was in the hospital. He got shot real bad with a shotgun. I called the doctor.

I said, "I want you to take good care of him. He's been with me a long time. Price is no object. I want him to have the best of care, any special attentions, special surgeon, you be sure."

"Well, [he] ain't going to live."

. . . "I want you to take care of him."

"Well, he ain't going to live . . ."

I said, "You don't know."

So I called up somebody else [to take care of him] and [he] didn't want to go there and interfere. . . . Anyway he got well.

## MARY WALTON'S CHURCH (Gene's sister-in-law)

*Sol:*

She worked for me forty-four years at the house—a long time. About two or three months before she got sick [she said], "Mr. Schulman, I want you to come to church. I want to show you what we need. We don't need much."

New air conditioning. New heat pump. New floors. New doors. Choir robes. OK.

So right then I told [the builder] get whatever she needs and send me the bill. So I fixed it up for about ten thousand dollars. You never saw such a happy woman in your life.

A few months later she died. I said to myself, "I don't want to see anybody die, but she died with a smile on her face."

## MARY WALTON TAKES SOL TO THE HOSPITAL

*Sol:*

When I got sick [and needed back surgery], I had to go to the hospital. How were we going to get me there? I said, "Mary will take me there." So I had this Cadillac. Instead of Mary driving it, I was driving us to the hospital.

*Gin Moses:*

You couldn't get into Mary's car. She called and asked what to do and told her to get you to the emergency room . . . so they made two or three stabs at getting into her little van and couldn't get in. He put her in his car, and here they go through town. He was driving and Mary was just sitting there.

## MARY WALTON THE CARETAKER

*Sol:*

They wanted to get a nurse for me [afterwards]. I don't want a nurse.

*Gin Moses:*

[He] said, "Mary will stay."

David and I had a nurse arranged. David sat in the yard while I came in to tell him. Mary said, "It won't work."

So we told him anyway and it didn't work. So Mary stayed with him at night. And then I got all the groceries and everything and helped her out. But he would get up of a morning and she would be in the other room with the door shut, sawing logs, and he'd get up and fix her breakfast and his breakfast.

*Sol:*

. . . That's what's called room service!

## MARY WALTON SETS SOL STRAIGHT

*Eds. Note: We were interviewing Milton Lurey, of Asheville, one of Sol's longtime friends, for another project and he told us this story about Sol and Mary:*

*Milton Lurey:*

After Sol's wife died, he told Mary that they no longer needed to keep kosher [observance of Jewish dietary laws]. Mary turned to him and said "Mr. Schulman, you *will* keep kosher as long as I am working for you."

## SURVEY LINES

*Sol:*

[A member of the church] came to me and said, "Sol, I belong to the Methodist Church, as you know. Next door to you. And you're a good neighbor. And we would like to buy eight to ten feet of your property.

As far as I know, I'm the only Jew who owns part of a Methodist Church. Anyway, I said, "How do I own part of your Methodist Church?

He said, "Well, we're on part of your land."

I had the land for years and years. They didn't know it until they went to survey something. . . .

So he said they needed eight to ten feet.

I said, "Sure you can have it."

"How much will it be?"

I said, "We'll talk about it."

This happened a little before [what I just told you]. He [had come] to me before they had told me about owning part of their land. [And he said] "Sol, would you consider selling your house?"

"Yeah, I'd consider most anything, what do you want me to consider?"

"Would you consider selling it?

"Yeah I sure would."

"How long would it take you to consider it?"

"Well, it might take me three or four minutes.

"Well, what did you decide?"

I told them, no, I wasn't interested in selling my house. But I was interested in buying the church.

After that I gave the church part of my land. I was glad to do it.

Same thing next door. . . . My neighbor had been living there over fifty years. She died. . . . Her daughter went to sell the house and she found a buyer. . . .

[They] came to me and said, "Sol, they've sold the house next door and we've got a problem."

I said, "What's your problem?"

"Her apartment is on your land. Not the whole thing. About eight, ten feet. We'd like to have it."

I said, "Well, you can have it."

"How much will it be?"

"Well, I'm going to charge you nothing."

So I gave it to them. So I had a blessing on both sides."

## SOL SCHULMAN DAY AT THE METHODIST CHURCH

*Reg Moody:*

So we thought it would be nice to honor him for his money that he'd give us for the parking lot and for giving us things, so we had a Sol Schulman Day at the First Methodist Church. And Herb and his whole family came. David, Herb and their families—everybody came. And we honored Sol Schulman.

And I kind of MC'd it and I said, "The reason we have Sol here today is because Sol owns our church." And everybody in the congregation got right quiet.

And I said, "Well, not all of it. Part of it. And he's giving it back to us today, and so we want to honor him." And he got a kick out of it.

And one comment that he did make to me following that little service, he said he just always thought the best looking women were at the synagogue, but since he came to the Methodist church, he wasn't so sure about that anymore.

## HELP TO FINLAND

*Sol:*

So they're collecting for this woman. [She works at Wal-Mart.] Her mother died in Finland. She had no way of getting there; had no money and they were out trying to collect some money. And *The Sylva Herald*, the newspaper people, they came to Gin and they said, "We need some money. Can you help us out a little bit? We need at least one thousand dollars to get [her] to Finland. She has no money and she doesn't know how she's going to get it."

Well, I've always liked to help people. My biggest mission in life is to have what they call in Jewish a "mitzvah," which is a blessing. And with a blessing you can live long. And they came to me and said, "Mr. Schulman can you help us out with five or ten dollars?"

"Yeah, I'll be glad to. How much money do you need?"

"We need a thousand dollars."

"How much you got?"

"We got about two hundred dollars."

So I wrote a check for a thousand dollars and gave it to them. Boy, you never saw a woman in your life started blessing me. It was worth ten million dollars just to hear somebody . . .

*Gin Moses:*

She didn't forget you either, did she? She brings him a cheesecake every year.

## THAT IS MARSHA CRITES?

*Marsha Crites [who stands about five feet four]:*

A really funny thing happened. As my daughters grew up, they would go in there to look for prom dresses or whatever, and one time—this was about six years ago—and my daughter went in to deliver a message from me.

And his assistant, maybe it was Gin, she called down—you know how he has that little box up there [the office] that he would stay in on the mezzanine—and she called up and said, "Mr. S. Come down here. You remember Marsha Crites, right?"

He said, "Sure, I remember Marsha Crites." And then he comes down and sees my very, very tall, blond, beautiful daughter and said, "*That* is Marsha Crites?!"

He thought I had had a transformation. So my daughter, Emily, and I laugh about that a lot. "*That* is Marsha Crites?"

## THE CADILLAC GETS AROUND

*Phyllis Foxx:*

Jim Bosworth was our director of the Main Street program [a small town revitalization program] and he got to know Mr. Schulman real well, and he'd stop in to see [him], you know. He baked bread, Mr. Bosworth did. He would bring us a loaf of bread or a pie or something . . . very often. And [he brought] Mr. Schulman and Gin some.

And he had to go to a Main Street program out of town and he didn't know if his little car was going to make it or not. He was having trouble with his car.

Mr. Schulman loaned Jim his Cadillac. And off Jim goes and it's coming a snow storm. . . . And he gets over on I-40 and there's been wrecks everywhere. And he spent a night, I think it was, in the car on I-40 sitting between here and Asheville, but he went on. I think the meeting was in Jacksonville, North Carolina.

He went on. He found a phone and called Mr. Schulman and told him he and the Cadillac were OK.

Now, how many people that you didn't know that well would you let go off in your Cadillac? Especially when they could have an accident and you be liable for the damages. I mean, Jim had been here less than a year when he did that. And he [Sol] didn't know him more than we did. . . .

## IT'S REMARKABLE

*Jan:*

So, do you have any feelings or experiences or comments about Sol being Jewish here since the thirties?

*Jack Hinson:*

It's a remarkable thing. I was so surprised. And I talked with him about that several times about how could he do that here. And he said that people are people anywhere you go and they basically—all of us need the same thing.

I agree with that! We all need a lot of attention and a lot of love and if we find somebody that can listen to us and give us that, we're going to be all right.

But I said, "Sol, you must have had a great deal of patience and determination to have done what you did." And he told me the story about being nineteen years old in 1933 and everybody knows that story.

But it's remarkable—it would have been good if he'd been a Baptist. But being Jewish—he might have been the first Jew in this whole place, in the whole town of Sylva. I don't know. I've never really researched that or looked into that too much. But I'm sure there weren't— there are not many here now—but I'm sure there weren't many.

But he and I always got along well. In fact he came . . . I believe he came, and David—I know David was there. I asked David to speak at our church one time when we were having a Seder meal. And David came and helped us with that, and we connected it with the Lord's Supper and with the Christian emphasis there.

So, I've always admired him and we've had great respect for each other and our different beliefs.

*Eds. Note: When Sol arrived in Sylva, there were already three other Jewish businessmen in town—Ben Lessing, Dave Karp and Abe Simon. [According to Susan Lewis, Lloyd Cowan and Abe Simon's nephew, Rabbi Michael Robinson.]*

# Chapter 3 – Customer Service Stories

## RACHEL PHILLIPS'S SWIMSUIT STORY

*Rachel Phillips:*

And in 1934 on the Fourth of July, they were having a big celebration in town. Having all kinds of contests, ball games, and half the county I think came to town that day. And that afternoon they were having this bathing suit contest at the Lyric Theatre, which is where Meriweather's is now.

And I was with Muriel Snyder who worked for Mr. Sol Schulman. And we met him on the street. And he said, "Are you girls going to be in the bathing suit contest?"

And we said, "No, we don't have a bathing suit!"

He took out his keys and handed them to Muriel Snyder. . . . Said, "You girls go out there and pick you out a bathing suit."

We came out to the store and, of course, we picked out the prettiest ones we could find. Mine was a one-piece—dark green and the top part was sort of a beige or light rose or something. Thought it was real pretty. So, then we went to the theatre and put our names in. That's all we had to do, give our name.

And I won the contest. Well, my mother didn't even know anything about it and she wasn't real happy. Her daughter's up there parading around at fifteen years old. But she simmered down pretty quick.

Mr. Schulman had already pledged to give ten dollars worth of merchandise. That's the way the prizes were, the merchants gave the prizes. But he didn't know at the time that it was going to be *more* than ten dollars, because he hadn't planned on the bathing suit! But anyways, so I used the ten dollars and I got a pair of shoes—sandals, real pretty—and beach pajamas.

So through the years, Sol and I have had a lot of fun kidding about it. One day he said, "You never did pay me for that bathing suit."

I said, "Oh all right I will, and I don't want to hear any more about it." I wrote a check for $2.98 and wrote a note and took it down and brought it up to him. And I said, "Now, here's the check and I don't want to hear any more about it."

And in the note I said—it's about two years ago I did this because I know I said, "Sixty-seven years ago I thought Mr. Schulman donated a bathing suit to me. But as the years have gone by, I have learned here he's started dunning me for that bathing suit [and that maybe he was hard up for money]. And I just got tired of hearing about it."

. . . And he got a big kick out of it.

And he said, “Well you still owe me the interest.”

And I said, “How much is that?”

“It’s eleven dollars.”

I said, “Look, you’re not getting it.”

And he tore the check up.

OK. When he was in the hospital I went by to speak to him.

He said, “You never did pay me that eleven dollars!”

So we’ve had a lot of fun through the years. The bathing suit really brought on a lot of joking about it.

## IMPERFECT PANTS

*Jack Hinson:*

When I was pastor at Cullowhee Baptist Church—I’d been here about a year or so—I came in here one day to just meet Sol. And he had some nice Sansabelt slacks [a brand of pants that do not need a belt] that I liked very much. I’d never bought any Sansabelt slacks.

He said, “Oh my, they’re wonderful. You ought to try ‘em if you’ve never had them on before.”

So I said “OK, I will.” So I went back there and I slipped them on and they felt so good. And they were a good price. And I came back out here and put them out on the counter and I really liked them. And when I looked on the inside I noticed that it had been rubber stamped and it said ‘imperfect.’

And I was surprised. I said, “Sol, these pants are imperfect.”

And just like that (snaps fingers), he said “Are you perfect?”

I said “No.”

He said, “These are for you.”

And I said, "Well, I'll take them then." So I bought that pair and I bought another pair—I bought three pair because I was imperfect, and they were good.

And that was Sol.

## SOL'S STYLE

*Jack Morris:*

I traded with Mr. Schulman for years. But one instance I remember in particular, I went in to buy a shirt. And I went in the left-hand door of the store. The shirts were all on the left. And the counter is along there with a glass top.

And I told Mr. Schulman I wanted a shirt, can't remember what type. But anyway, he got behind the counter and started pulling shirts down. Here's one, here's another type. And he had the whole counter piled high with shirts.

You felt obligated to buy, he'd gone so far out of his way to help you. But I just remember that in particular. Just about every shirt on the shelf he had lying down on the counter for me to look at.

*Woman shopper:*

I shopped in here so many years ago. He was sweet because if you didn't have enough money, you know, like for something, he'd give it to you for what you had. Very sweet.

## BED JACKET – VERSION 1

*David Schulman:*

The most memorable story was that Dean W. B. Harrill [of Western Carolina University] would show up each December and buy his wife a bed jacket [a jacket-length robe]. The same bed jacket. The phenomenon would occur because he would buy this half robe and we would wrap it for Christmas for him to give to his wife, but each January Mrs. Harrill would surreptitiously return it for something that she really wanted and we would put the bed jacket—the only one we ever carried—and put it back in stock. The real mystery is what did he think his wife did with the jacket between January and December? [This went on for 30 years.]

## BED JACKET – VERSION 2

*Sol:*

One of the professors at Western—very nice man—every year like clockwork at Christmas time, he'd come in for a gift for his wife. Always the same thing. "I want the prettiest bed jacket to give to my wife."

Every year when [he] would come by, we knew he'd come by for a bed jacket. He died about eight or ten years ago. His wife called me up about a year after he died.

"Mr. Schulman, can I see you?"

"Yeah, come on by this afternoon."

"OK."

[When she came in she said] "You know my dear husband, he was such a wonderful person"

I said, "I know it."

"I miss him terribly."

I said, "I know it. What's on your mind?"

"Well, you know he bought me these beautiful bed jackets. For thirty years straight, every year he bought me a bed jacket. I never put one on in my life. I don't even know how you put one on!"

I said, "OK, then I'll take it back."

I quit selling bed jackets 40-50 years ago. . . . Every year for thirty years, she put it away. Every year he bought the same one. She never put one on. That's meshuganah [Yiddish for "crazy"].

## THE BALD SPOT

*David Schulman:*

Dean Harrill would pass by our three-way mirror in the store and then turn and tell anyone who was handy, such as my mother, dad, brother and me, that he never knew he was developing a bald spot on the back of his head until he looked into our mirror, and he would tell this story for at least thirty years. My brother and I would brace ourselves for another round and smile as he repeated his story. We would smile and listen with virgin ears as if we never heard the story before.

## SHOE SWAP

*Sol:*

One of the professors, not too long before I closed down—bought Florsheim shoes once about every five years—he'd come to me, bought a pair of Florsheim shoes. Store was packed, it was busy. I was the only [one] back there who could sell men's shoes.

. . . He came back the next day and said, "Sol, I would like a favor."

"OK."

"The shoes you sold me are wonderful. I love them, I love the style, the color. I love everything about them. But they're a little bit too small. Could you give me one a little bit bigger?"

So I said, "Yeah, I'd be glad to. I've got a customer now." He had a newspaper under his arm.

[I said] "Sit down in the chair, read your newspaper and I'll be with you in five or ten minutes."

Well, about ten minutes, maybe fifteen minutes I was with another customer. Then I go out to wait on [him] and he's gone. . . . Must have felt insulted. Why didn't he wait for me? I felt very bad about it. That he wouldn't wait.

A week or two later I see the guy in the post office.

"Sol, I got those shoes you swapped for me. They're so comfortable! I never had a more comfortable shoe in my life."

I never swapped them, I never touched them.

## GOING TO THE LAKE

*Phyllis Foxx:*

Well, I remember Mr. Schulman from when I was a girl coming to town. You know, I always loved to come in here to shop. He and his wife were both here. That would have been in the 1950s. I graduated from high school in 1960 and that's when I went to work in town. . . . He sold me my first bathing suit. It was beautiful.

. . . I grew up when we weren't suppose to wear shorts and bathing suits and so on. Well, I finally got brave (and my sister-in-law still asks about the first time I wore shorts). I was going to the lake and I'd never had a bathing suit. Dad took us to the lake all the time, but we did not have bathing suits. We wore jeans or pants.

I was going with a friend to the lake and we were going with two guys and so I wanted a bathing suit. And I had seen Mr. Schulman's bathing suits in the window. You know, Jantzen. They were so pretty, I thought.

I came in and I tried [some] on and I picked out red and white gingham. It wasn't stretchy. It was the shorts with the underpants, you know. And the top—it wasn't bikini—it came to my midriff. I kept that bathing suit. I bet I kept that bathing suit twenty years. I thought that was the prettiest bathing suit I'd ever seen.

I still think it was the prettiest and the nicest bathing suit. I've bought a lot of bathing suits, but I've never had one that I enjoyed as much as the first one. Seems like it was $17.95. It was a week's pay almost, but it lasted twenty years.

I had other bathing suits during that time, but I just could not get rid of that bathing suit. Gradually, the sun just drew the red out. I can see that bathing suit just like it was laying there on the table.

So, he sold me my first bathing suit.

## SOL'S KNEE

*Jack Hinson:*

When I came in here—he talked so fast, you know, Sol talked real fast. I said, "Sol, how you doing?"

He said, "Well I'm doing all right. How you doing?"

I said, "I'm fine. I noticed you limping."

He said, "Yeah I've got a bad knee, a bad knee."

I said, "Well, what's wrong with your knee."

He said, "I don't know. I went to the doctor and he told me it was old age, but I told him it couldn't be old age because the other knee was the same age and it wasn't hurting."

## BEAUTY QUEEN COAT

*Rena Ensley:*

My daughter . . . was going to school out at Southwestern Tech [STI]. So she . . . became the queen at STI. So she got to ride the float through town during the Christmas Parade.

So Mr. Schulman he loaned her this—it was a real cold—and he loaned her this coat.

It was a beautiful coat with fur around it—beige. So, she wore it during the parade here, and then in Canton and in Asheville. And then she brought it back. He loaned it to her.

I thought that was real neat. I have a clipping at home somewhere, but I can't find it. I don't know where to look for it at. But I thought that was neat. Her name is Gay Ensley Wilkes and she lives at Cullowhee.

## SOL PAYS ATTENTION

*Jack Hinson:*

If you walked in here, you feel like you're somebody—he makes you feel that way. He remembers your size. I would come in here, and he would say, "Well, Jack I saw where you had a funeral [as a pastor] last week."

I said, "Sol how do you remember all that stuff?"

"Well, I just saw it in the paper."

It wasn't anything to him. That's just who he was. I just think it's really wonderful.

## WEDDING

*Kathy Watkins:*

And then when my husband and I got married, we got the tux down here and so we come that day to pick up the tux which was August 1, 1987. And it was so hot that day and Mr. Schulman come up and says, "Honey, it's so hot today if you can't afford to get a church or to get married in a church. I'll pay for it for you so you can have air conditioning."

My father-in-law says, "I'd sure help him pay for it." [Laughter] But for him to want to help pay for our wedding 'cause it was so hot that day. And we wished afterward that we'd let him because we did burn up. It was an outside wedding.

## AN ESPECIALLY JOYOUS CHRISTMAS

*Rachel Phillips:*

I think it was about Christmas, 1940. My brother came to me on Christmas Eve and gave me some money and said, "I want you to do my Christmas shopping. Buy Mother a waffle iron."

He'd been someplace and had waffles and really liked them, so he thought that would be a really nice gift to give Mother. So I got the waffle iron at the Sylva Pharmacy which was located where Hollifield Jewelers are now. And then I was rushing around.

And back then, half the people waited until Christmas Eve to do their shopping and the stores stayed open until ten o'clock or later. So I was rushing around getting gifts for him.

And I was downstairs at Schulman's—I don't remember what I got down there. But anyway, I went home. And later we were going to take our aunts' gifts to them, which was a tradition on Christmas Eve. We'd go there late and take them their gifts.

When I started to get my pocketbook, I couldn't find it. Well, I was right upset about it because I had fifteen dollars that I'd saved for my Christmas shopping and I was so proud that I had fifteen dollars left.

And so I thought, well the last place I was at was Schulman's. So I called Mr. Schulman [at home] and asked him if anyone had turned a pocketbook in. And he said no, but he would check the next morning. And so he went in the next morning.

And I went up to my husband's grandparents for dinner. And I was in the house and my husband was outside with the men. And then my husband came walking in and had my pocketbook. Sol had gone Christmas morning to the store and found the pocketbook downstairs where I said I was. And he called my mother and she told him that we were up at Willets—that's on the way to Asheville. And so Sol brought my pocketbook to me.

And I really had a very nice Christmas then because I was pretty upset over losing that fifteen dollars in my pocketbook. So, he's just done many wonderful things for people all his life.

## WEDDING DRESS

*Sol:*

A woman came to the store. . . . She wants to buy a wedding dress. . . . [It cost] maybe a hundred, a hundred fifty dollars. She kept paying it down with five dollars, ten dollars. Maybe about a year or so later, it was still on layaway.

A man came to the store—he'd been drinking. Said, "Are you the owner of this store?"

I said, "Yeah."

"My girlfriend," he said, "paid eighty dollars, ninety dollars on a wedding dress. She wants her money back." Well we don't want to give money back, not after keeping it on layaway so long.

I said, "You don't deserve it." Oh he blessed me out, it was terrible.

Gin always used to come to my aid. So she said, "Don't get excited. Don't start cursing. You don't deserve anything back. But tell her whatever she paid down on the dress, we'll give to her in merchandise." That's what she did.

So twenty years later . . .

*Gin Moses:*

No, it wasn't that long. It was several years [later] that you saw him at . . .

*Sol:*

Saw him at Wal-Mart. I was parking my car. He came to me and said, "Are you Sol Schulman?"

I didn't recognize the guy. "Yeah."

He said, "I owe you an apology."

I said, "What for?" I always accept apologies and don't even ask for them, but I want to know what's this for.

He said, "I acted like an ass, if you'll excuse the expression. I know I was wrong and I'd been drinking. I didn't marry that bitch anyway. I owe you an apology."

## ONE-HUNDRED-YEAR-OLD MAN – VERSION 1

*Sol:*

Tell you one that was in the article they had in the newspaper. About this man who came in and bought a suit. Had five sons. Never had a suit in his life and he's sixty-five years old. A deputy sheriff. Came in with his five boys. Not boys—the youngest boy must have been fifty or forty.

"Can we buy a suit for fifty dollars? Each one of us will pay ten dollars to buy Dad a suit—he's never had one."

I said, "Sure, we can do that." In those days fifty dollars was a lot of money.

So he bought the suit and he looks in the mirror and says, "Boy I look good, don't I?"

"Yeah, you look good."

He went to the door and he said, "How long will this suit last me?"

"Don't worry, it will last you. It will last 'til you get to be a hundred."

"It'll last that long? "

"I'll tell you what I'll do. I'll guarantee you. When you're a hundred years old—you're sixty-five now—I'll give you a suit. . . . "

Five years later he came by and says, "Remember me?"

"No, who are you?" He reminded me and I said OK.

"I'm seventy years old and you promised me a suit when I get to be a hundred."

"If I promised you a suit, don't worry about it, you'll get one."

Five years later, he's seventy-five. "Remember me?" I can't remember everybody in the store.

He says, "I'm so-and-so and you promised me a suit when I get to be a hundred. . . . " This went on every five years. When he got to be ninety he called me. Came into the store. One of his sons brought him to me and said, "He wants to talk to you in private." Well, what could be private? I said, "OK. Come on back here."

"No, I want it in private." It wasn't private enough.

"What can I do for you?"

"Have you made arrangements?"

"Arrangements for what?"

"Suppose you die before I get my suit? Who's going to give me my suit? I want to know if you've made arrangements."

I said, "OK." To cut it off short, I read [his obituary] in the paper one morning and here he is, so-and-so, almost a hundred—ninety-nine—and would have been a hundred in a few days. So I said to myself, "Gee whiz.

I do remember I made him a promise and I'm going to keep my promise."

So I call Reg Moody's grandfather [director of the funeral home]. "Mr. Moody, I've got a problem. Well, not a problem, but I promised this man a suit of clothes when he got to be a hundred. And he died yesterday only lacking a few weeks. Send one of your men and I want them to pick out a suit, shirt and so on."

"Can't do it."

"Why not?"

"Well," he said, "Once you dress a body you can't take off the garment and put it on somebody else."

I said, "I've got to do something because I promised that man a suit." Not that I'm such a hero. . . . But I've got to do something for that man. Well I got to thinking, thinking, thinking.

So I call Mr. Moody, and said, "Moody, did he have enough insurance to pay for his funeral?"

"No. He's got three hundred dollars worth of insurance." [You] pay all your life for three hundred dollars. "Needs two hundred dollars, but I guess we'll get it from the family."

I said, "No, I'll pay for it." I sent him a check for two hundred dollars.

That night I went to bed and got to thinking and there's that man laying in the coffin and he's dead! But he's looking straight at me, his eyes are open. "You promised me a suit. Thank you, I got it."

## ONE-HUNDRED-YEAR-OLD MAN – VERSION 2

*Reg Moody:*

. . . I came to Sylva from Bryson City in 1964 to operate this funeral home. And I found out very shortly after I got here that we sold burial suits. And our burial suits, of course, the backs weren't sewn up in them. . . . And so some people didn't like that. So instead of buying a suit from us, they would go up the street and buy the clothes for the men, especially the men, from Sol.

And they never did come back that they said, "Well we bought the suit and Mr. Schulman gave us the shirt and tie." He always gave somebody something when they'd go in there.

*Sharon:*

Did he do that at other times, like if people couldn't afford their burial clothes?

*Reg Moody:*

Yeah, if they couldn't afford the clothes, he would give 'em to them.

*Jan:*

But usually people he knew, or not necessarily?

*Reg Moody:*

Well, most of the time he knew them. But Sol just found out that someone was having difficulty, he'd call them and tell them they could come get the clothes and he wouldn't charge them anything for them. Sol loved to help people at a time like that.

One of the funniest stories that he told me is this man went in there and traded with Sol. And Sol told him, "You know when you die I'm going to give you your burial clothes. I'm going to furnish them. I'm going to take them down to Moody's when you die."

So the man said, "OK."

And every time he'd go into the store, he'd remind Sol of his promise to give him his burial clothes. Well Sol said he just kind of up and died all of a sudden and by the time he heard about it and got involved in it, they'd already had other clothes and had him dressed and in the casket ready for the funeral and everything.

And he called my grandfather, P. E. Moody, and he said, "P. E., you've got so-and-so down there."

And he [P. E.] said,"Yeah."

He said, "Well, I'm suppose to furnish his burial clothes."

And granddaddy said, "It's too late. Everything's already set and we're ready to go." And so he said, "Well I tell you what I'm going to do. I'm going to pay a hundred dollars toward his funeral expenses because I promised him that I would help with his burial clothes."

Of course, Mr. Moody didn't hesitate to take the hundred dollars toward the expense of it, you know. So that's one of the stories about him furnishing clothes when people died. But he did that right on up for people who bought clothes from him.

*Jan:*

Did that man happen to be a sheriff for Jackson County? Do you know who it was?

*Reg Moody:*

I don't remember. . . . Have you heard the story?

*Jan:*

He told us a story that was actually that story inside out. The way that he told us the story was that the man asked him if it was a good suit.

"Yeah, it's a good suit."

"Will it last a long time?"

"Yeah, it will last a long time."

"Will it last until I'm a hundred?"

And Sol said, "When you're a hundred you come in and I'll give you a suit." And then every five years he'd come in and say, "I'm the person."

*Reg Moody:*

That's right. That's the same story. . . .

*Sharon:*

But it's good to hear it from another side. Yeah, we've got it from the salesman's side and we've got it from the burial-man's side.

*Jan:*

It's a great example of the same story being told by different people.

## DIAMONDS

*Kathy Watkins:*

[My mother] had come down here to buy her a dress to wear to her [fiftieth] class reunion, a special dress. Well, she found her a special outfit to wear to her class reunion and Mr. Schulman says, "Oh, wait a minute. I've got something for you."

So he left and went upstairs and come back down with a diamond necklace and diamond earrings and says, "Take this. I want you to wear this to your class reunion with this new outfit and bring it back to me when you get through using them."

And she did. And everybody just thought they were beautiful, but for somebody to do something—of course he's known mother all her life, too, or since he's been here, but still just to do that for somebody. To give them diamonds to wear was something special. . . .

They came from upstairs. I am sure they were probably his wife's. This was after she had passed away, but for somebody to let someone wear diamonds—that was really special.

## THE WINDOWS ON MAIN STREET

*Marsha Crites:*

The items in the window very rarely changed over the years, and for the young people around it's like, "Oh my gosh! Is this a vintage store or a real store or what?"

But it was almost something of a comfort to walk by the window because it was the one thing you could count on—that the same ladies' dresses and shoes would be there, no matter what the styles were. And occasionally he would change the dress. But it would be the same kind of dress.

But there won't be any more windows like that in Sylva now that Sol's store is gone. And it's kind of sad for me.

# PART III
# Appendices

# Appendix A – Honorary Doctorate Speech

*This is a speech given by Chancellor John W. Bardo of Western Carolina University about Sol Schulman on December 14, 2002, when he was given an honorary doctorate from Western Carolina University.*

Sol Schulman, visionary entrepreneur, exemplary businessman, civic leader, and wellspring of wit, of wisdom, and of benevolence, you have fashioned a legacy of service, of spirit, and of hard work that stands as a beacon to those who will continue to strive for the American Dream.

Seven decades ago, in January of 1933, in the midst of the Great Depression, you opened a retail store in Sylva. Though only nineteen years of age and with a perilously thin financial base, you had the courage, the vision, and some say the audacity, to launch a new business in a small mountain town. Many doubted you. Many predicted failure and stepped forward to advise you that you had no chance of surviving in such hard times. Many were wrong.

You worked hard. You worked smart. And most notably, you worked with a guiding principle that by providing customers with the merchandise they needed and by treating them honestly and fairly, you would succeed. And succeed you did. Schulman's Department Store became a landmark on Main Street in Sylva and operated continuously in the same building for almost seventy years. Schulman's exemplifies your work ethic and became recognized and admired not just in Jackson County, but around the globe. When you retired, at age ninety, there were no more naysayers of Sol Schulman or his business.

Always public minded, you were sought and served willingly in public services and philanthropy. Twice after age eighty, when others would have declined, you served terms on the Sylva Town Board. Through the years, you held leadership roles for Wachovia Bank, C. J. Harris Hospital and the Jackson County Community Foundation. You were president of the Sylva Merchants Association and the Jackson County Chamber of Commerce and the chairman of the Fontana Regional Library.

You measured thousands of customers in your store, recalling suit sizes, inseams and sleeve lengths with astounding accuracy. But you also measured people in other ways. You took the measure of their humanity, their needs and their value as fellow human beings and neighbors. Quick to size but not to criticize, you were an astute observer. There were no barriers of faith, persuasion or rank when it came to your willingness to assist others in need.

Measuring the needs of your neighbors, your community and often, Western Carolina University, you stepped forward time after time with quiet generosity and quiet benevolence, for which you sought neither public notice nor acclaim. Often the financial assistance you provided was known only by those directly involved in the transactions, albeit the benefits were often profound and far-reaching. A long-time friend and colleague said it best—Sol Schulman knows the value of money, but he places a lot more value on people.

As a benefactor, supporter and friend of Western Carolina University, you have an impeccable record. In the archives that chronicle many of the university's major milestones, again and again, there surfaces documentation of your commitment and undergirding support. There are scholarship milestones, athletics milestones, new programs to assist the University, such as the original Patrons of Quality and the New Century Scholars, that bear your mark. And in the record of these many milestones, often one will find a handwritten note saying simply, "Do not need to be identified as it is a pleasure to help," signed Sol Schulman.

As you, Sol Schulman, have measured your fellow human beings, in so many ways, for so many years; today, we take the measure of a lifetime of achievements, of distinguished service, of citizenship, of friendship, of compassion and of caring. Your empathy for humanity and willingness to help others embodies the spirit of what this university is all about. In recognition of your accomplishments, and for your significant contributions to build the university and community, the Board of Trustees of Western Carolina University is pleased to award, and the Chancellor to confer, the degree of Doctor of Humane Letters, Honoris Causa, at this Commencement Ceremony on December 14, 2002, with all the rights and privileges appertaining.

# Appendix B – Suggested Bibliography

Epstein, Howard. *Jews in Small Towns: Legends and Legacies*. Santa Rosa, CA: Vision Books International, 1997.

Evans, Eli. *The Provincials: A Personal History of the Jews in the South*. New York: Atheneum, 1976.

Finkelstein, Leo. *Leo Finkelstein's Asheville and The Poor Man's Bank*. Boone, NC: The Center for Appalachian Studies, 1998.

Golden, Harry. *Our Southern Landsman*. New York: G. P. Putnam, 1974.

Jackson County Heritage, North Carolina. *The Heritage of Jackson County*. Marceline, MO and Waynesville, NC: Jackson County Genealogical Society, Volume I, 1992, Volume II, 2000.

Kaganoff, Nathan and Melvin Urofsky, eds. *Turn to the South: Essays on Southern Jewry*. Charlottesville, VA: University Press of Virginia, 1977.

Rogoff, Leonard. *Homelands: Southern Jewish Identity in Durham and Chapel Hill, NC*. Tuscaloosa, AL and London: The University of Alabama Press, 2001.

Weinstein, Maurice, ed. *Zebulon Vance and "The Scattered Nation."* Charlotte, NC: Wildacres Press, 1995.

Williams, Max R. ed. *The History of Jackson County*. Sylva, North Carolina: Jackson County Historical Association, 1987.

# Appendix C - Storytellers

The following people were interviewed:
*(Those with asterisks have stories included in this book.)*

**Howard Allman*** – grew up in Sylva, got his only two suits from Sol
**Evelyn Austin** – wife of Gene Austin who worked for the Schulman's for many years
**Robert Brooks** – local customer
**Gary Carden** – local writer and storyteller
**Martha Coward** – Sylva resident and customer
**Lloyd Cowan*** – local and former manager of Belks store located in downtown Sylva
**Marsha Crites*** – Senior Associate, Special Projects for the Jackson County Community Foundation
**Matt Davis** – Seventeen, first time in store when it was closing
**Michele Garashi Ellick** – lives in Sylva and is the Foundation Director for WestCare Health System
**Dr. N. R. El Bayadi** – served on several boards with Sol
**Josie Ellis** – lifelong customer
**Rena Ensley*** – Sylva resident and customer
**Ed Finch** – retired, recently moved to area from Norfolk, Virginia, where there was another Schulman family store
**Phyllis Foxx*** – business owner in downtown Sylva
**Jack Hinson*** – former pastor at Cullowhee Baptist Church
**Livingston Kelley*** —business owner since 1978 next door to Schulman's
**Milton Lurey*** – long-time friend of Sol's
**Susan Lewis** – neighbor and close family friend of the Schulmans
**Peggy Medford** – shopper
**Reg Moody*** – local funeral home director
**John H. (Jack) Morris, Jr.*** – downtown business owner, lifetime resident of Sylva and customer of Schulman's
**Virginia (Gin) Moses*** – former employee and close friend of the Schulmans
**Brenda Oliver** – Mayor of Sylva
**Rachel Phillips*** – beauty pageant winner and customer of Sol's
**David Schulman*** —younger son of Sol and Lillian Schulman
**Herbert Schulman** – older son of Sol and Lillian Schulman
**Sol Schulman*** – subject of this book; shop owner in downtown Sylva for seventy years
**Kathy Watkins*** – customer from Webster

# Appendix D - Index

# Appendix E – Photos and Illustrations

| | |
|---|---|
| Cover | Sylva, 1951, courtesy of *The Sylva Herald;* Schulman's Department Store logo, copyright © 2003 Jan Schochet; Young Sol photo from the Schulman Collection; current Sol photo copyright © 2003 Jan Schochet. |
| Page iii | Top photo: Sol, Lillian, Herbert and David Schulman at Herbert's bar mitzvah in Beth Israel Synagogue in Asheville, NC, 1956, Schulman Collection. Bottom: Sol, left, and Herbert, holding the Torah, at Herbert's bar mitzvah (see above). |
| Page vi | Advertisements from *The Sylva Herald:* Top, January 11, 1951 and Bottom, March 10, 1955. |
| Page x | Postcard of Sylva, n.d., copyright © Asheville Post Card Co.<br>Map, copyright © Mapquest.com, Inc. |
| Page 1 | I. S. Schulman's Store, Cherryville, NC, Sol Schulman, Irvin Samuel Schulman (Sol's father) and employee. ca. 1929-1930, Schulman Collection. |
| Page 4 | Schulman's Department Store logo, Schulman Collection. Sol's high school graduation picture, Reidsville, NC, 1929, Schulman Collection. |
| Page 5 | President Franklin D. Roosevelt visits Sylva, NC, September 9, 1936, courtesy of *The Sylva Herald.* |
| Page 12 | Sol Schulman home, designed 1938 by Charles Parker, architect of the Grove Arcade, Asheville, NC, copyright ©2003 Jan Schochet. |
| Page 13 | Lloyd Cowan, sixteen, modeling his first pair of swim trunks, purchased at Schulman's. They cost $1.98 plus tax. Caption on photograph reads: "Sol's swim suit brings out the best of Lloyd." Location, East Fork Rd., Sylva, NC, 1938. Courtesy Lloyd Cowan. |
| Page 20 | Sol's Cadillac. Copyright © 2003 Jan Schochet. |
| Page 21 | David Schulman's birthday party - from left to right: Rebecca and Dave Karp, Susan Lessing (now Lewis), David Schulman, Sophia and Ben Lessing, Lillian and Sol Schulman, at the Schulman house on Jackson Street in Sylva, NC, ca. 1954. Schulman Collection. |
| Page 23 | Advertisements from *The Sylva Herald:* Left, February 7, 1945 and Right, January 24, 1945. |
| Page 34 | Schulman's Department Store Bicentennnial display window, 1976. Schulman Collection. |
| Page 35 | Background screen photo, Main Street, Sylva, NC, ca. 1950s. Courtesy *The Sylva Herald.* Photo of Sylva's Country Harvest Festival celebrants, ca. 1980s. Left to right: Lloyd Cowan (manager of Belk's), Bob Porter (locksmith), Sol Schulman, unknown, Bill Henderson (worked at radio station), who is wearing a blue ribbon that he likely won in the hog-calling or tobacco-spitting contest. (Sol's son, David, started this promotion when he was president of the Sylva Merchants' Association. David had six David's and Boo-Boos Outlets stores in Western North Carolina). Schulman Collection. |
| Page 38 | Schulman's Department Store second story façade. Copyright © 2003 Jan Schochet. |
| Page 44 | Sylva Main Street, August 2003. Copyright © 2003 Jan Schochet. |

# About the Editors

**Jan Schochet** is an Asheville native whose family has lived in Asheville and owned downtown businesses there since the 1880s. She, too, has worked in those businesses. In addition, she earned a M.A. in Folklore, wrote her master's thesis on teaching Jewish family folklore and owned and ran a company that took clients on folklore-based trips of the Carolinas. She is nearing completion of an M.F.A. in film and video production and has collected oral histories for the *Down Home Project: A History of the Jews of North Carolina.*

**Sharon Fahrer** is an environmental planner turned historian. She has worked in her family's business, the fourth generation to do so. While always interested in history, her career in consulting and nonprofit organizations did not provide an opportunity to be a history sleuth. Then she moved to a historic house in the National Register district of Montford in Asheville, North Carolina, joined the board of the Asheville-Buncombe Preservation Society and became hooked on history. She has collected family oral histories as well as histories for the *Down Home Project: A History of the Jews of North Carolina.*

Jan and Sharon are independent historians and, working under the name of History@Hand, they collect oral histories of families, communities and businesses for their clients. If you would like more information about History@Hand call (828) 253-0982 or email: fahrer@charter.net.

*If you are interested in making a tax-deductible donation to the Schulman Family Fund, mail your gift to the Jackson County Community Foundation, P.O. Box 2148, Sylva, NC. For more information about the project, call Marsha Crites at (828) 631-3872 or Sue LeLievre at (828) 586-4616. To order additional copies of this book, call (828) 253-0982 or email fahrer@charter.net.*

SCHULMAN
FOR RENT
Schulman's
DEPT. STORE
Livingston's
PHOTO

Made in the USA
Monee, IL
29 November 2019

Therefore, implementing the Montessori pedagogy in your home will help you raise your toddler without hindrances and deviations. This book will explore:

- The basic history and principles of the Montessori method
- The traits of an absorbent mind and sensitive periods
- The possible obstacles to development in the early years
- Importance of movement and language acquisition
- The preparation of Montessori-friendly home and the proper equipment
- Montessori subjects and setting up the learning corners
- Montessori inspired lessons and exercises to be implemented at home
- Details of the didactic material and its significance
- The parents as teachers of a Montessori toddler and their role
- *And much more...*